The Passive Income Blueprint Affiliate Marketing Edition

Create Passive Income with Ecommerce using Shopify, Amazon FBA, Affiliate Marketing, Retail Arbitrage, eBay and Social Media

By

Income Mastery

damages, or monetary loss due to the information herein, either directly or indirectly.

Respective authors own all copyrights not held by the publisher.

The information herein is offered for informational purposes solely, and is universal as so. The presentation of the information is without contract or any type of guarantee assurance.

The trademarks that are used are without any consent, and the publication of the trademark is without permission or backing by the trademark owner. All trademarks and brands within this book are for clarifying purposes only and are the owned by the owners themselves, not affiliated with this document.

Table of Contents

Introduction

There are many different ways to make money online, but affiliate marketing is one of the oldest and most time-tested forms out there! Through creating high-quality websites that have good content, you can refer hundreds of people to products and collect a hefty commission for each product sold. Best of all, you don't have to own a single product! Instead, you simply join an affiliate program, post links and wait for your website visitors to click on them, collecting a profit each time someone makes a purchase!

Affiliate marketing is easy to learn but hard to master. This book will help you learn all of the ins and outs of affiliate marketing, teaching you everything you need to become successful in this online business. If you have an entrepreneurial spirit and want to get involved with an online business that has near unlimited income potential, then affiliate marketing is for you!

Chapter 1: What is Affiliate Marketing?

Affiliate marketing is one of the oldest forms of online marketing, and if you do it right, it can be quite lucrative. So what is affiliate marketing? Simply put, it is the process of referring potential customers to another business and then collecting a commission based on traffic or sales that were generated by your referral.

Marketing tends to be one of the biggest challenges for any business, whether online or offline. By offering an affiliate program, a business essentially entrusts the affiliate to do the bulk of the marketing work, in exchange for a financial reward. It is useful for both parties, as the business doesn't need to shell out money for marketing upfront and the affiliate marketer can make money for all of his efforts.

In this chapter, we'll be exploring both the history of affiliate marketing, as well as how the business model itself functions.

The History of Affiliate Marketing

The idea of paying for referrals is not unique to the internet. It has existed within the business world for hundreds of years. However, the concept of affiliate marketing online is almost as old as the internet itself. First patented in 1989 by William J. Tobin, owner of the PC Flowers and Gifts company, affiliate marketing allowed for eCommerce endeavors to grow exponentially. With PC Flowers and Gifts offering bounties to marketers who referred people to their products and services, they were able to make over $6 million a year!

Other businesses would look at this model and quickly find their own ways to incorporate it. Amazon created an associate program in 1996, paying out commissions whenever a customer is visiting a referral link purchased on their website. Considering the size of Amazon's offerings, this enables affiliate marketers to grow the diversity of what they were advertising on their websites.

As a practice, affiliate marketing quickly grew over the years. Savvy entrepreneurs who were looking to make money online realized that the possibilities of income growth were nearly endless. They worked to innovate their websites, creating more attractive ways to draw in potential customers.

They focused on creating good content and product reviews, as a way to organically generate more traffic. Those who were successful made quite a bit of money. In 2006, it was estimated that over $6 billion had been paid out in commissions to affiliates.

While the majority of the internet has changed, and new fads rise and fall quickly, affiliate marketing hasn't gone anywhere. Even today, affiliate marketing remains as one of the most popular ways to run an online business, and with more and more companies getting involved, the potential for getting paid is higher than ever!

The Bussines Model of Affiliate Marketing

The actual business model of affiliate marketing is simple. A business, referred to as an advertiser, offers a type of reward for traffic or sales of a product. These rewards can range from pay-per-click, in which the advertiser pays out whenever someone clicks on a link, revenue sharing, where they pay out a percentage of the sale that was made, or cost per mile, where they pay for every 1000 people who have viewed their affiliate link.

The affiliate hosts these links on their website, either as banner ads or organically within articles that they have written. Tracking systems allow for advertisers to be able to tell where link clicks came from, so if a customer clicks on an affiliate's link, the advertiser has access to that information. It is crucial because if a customer clicks on a link and then makes a sale, the affiliate is credited with that sale and thus earns the commission.

At the end of the day, it is in an affiliate's best interest to create methods of drawing in people to their website, so that they can generate more traffic towards their affiliate links. A percentage of that traffic will buy, also known as convert, and in the process, make the affiliate more money.

Don't be fooled by the simplicity of the affiliate marketing model. While it is really just a three-step process (create a link, offer the link, wait for the customer to click and buy), you will face a host of challenges. Getting started as an affiliate marketer is easy; however, making money is the hard part.

The Roles

In affiliate marketing, there are three parties involved at all times. The publisher, the advertising, and the customer. Let's take a look at each profile more in-depth.

The Advertiser

The advertiser is the one who offers the affiliate the bounty. There are many different types of advertisers that you will come across in the affiliate marketing world. Some advertisers run their affiliate operation, while others may opt to work with an affiliate network, providing bounties to a large group of affiliates at a time. Some advertisers are so big that they created their type of affiliate network and others are so small that they only work with very specific individuals.

While the nature of an advertiser may vary, their goals are all the same: they want people visiting their websites and buying their products. Finding an advertiser isn't very difficult, and in the fourth chapter, we'll review different programs that are offered by various advertisers.

The Customer

The customer's role is simple; all they need to do is visit your website, click your affiliate links and purchase the products that they find. However, the difficulty lies in getting them to convert. It is important to remember that only a small portion of your traffic will be the ones to actually make the purchases or click on the links. Learning how to persuade them to move from being interested in making the final purchase is one of the most vital tasks for an affiliate marketer to learn.

The Publisher

An affiliate is a publisher. They publish content for specific products, in the hopes of gaining a link click. It means that if you want to be an affiliate, you will have to learn how to think like a website marketer. You can't just create a simple website and throw up a few links, hoping for the best. Instead, you'll need to develop a content strategy that will help bring in targeted traffic that will clink on the links that you have to offer.

A publisher's main job is to drive traffic to their website. The traffic must be high quality, full of the target demographic who would want to purchase the products that you are advertising in your banners. It doesn't matter how big of an audience you have, and if they are outside of your target demographic, you won't see conversions.

Quiz

1. The name of the company that actually sells the product is called:
   a. Publisher
   b. Advertiser
   c. Seller
   d. Retailer
2. Affiliate marketing has a tremendous start-up cost
   a. True
   b. False
3. What is the publisher's role in affiliate marketing?
   a. Purchase the product
   b. Create links to products in the hopes of seeing a sale
   c. Buy a product and then resell it on their own website
4. A publisher collects a commission when
   a. The customer engages in a specific action (buying or clicking a link)
   b. The customer visits the publisher's website
   c. The customer shares the publisher's content.

Chapter 2: What is Low Ticket and High Ticket Affiliate Marketing?

Sometimes you might hear someone refer to an expensive item as a high ticket item. In affiliate marketing, high ticket refers to products that sell for high commissions. Low ticket applies to smaller commissions.

When it comes to affiliate marketing, you're the one who is in control of the type of products and advertisers that you work with. You can choose between offering low ticket items, focusing on volume but collecting smaller commissions, or you can choose to focus on high ticket items, which will sell less, but you'll obtain a significantly larger commission each time.

Let's review the pros and cons of both types of commission structures

Low Ticket Affiliate Marketing

Low ticket means either the price on the products are so low that the commissions will be small, or that the advertiser isn't offering a large commission percentage. Either way, the payout for each conversion will be relatively small.

The advantages of low ticket marketing lie within volume. If you can generate a large amount of traffic on your website on a monthly basis, you may find more success offering low ticket items. The smaller price point of these low ticket items means that more people will convert. So if you are selling a product for $5.00 on your website, and you have 1,000 people a month convert, you would be selling $5,000 a month. If you have a decent commission structure, you could be taking between 40 percent of that 5,000, which could leave you ultimately with 2,000 a month. Of course, this assumes you have a generous commission structure.

The disadvantages lie within your commission rate. If you are collecting a low commission, combined with low product costs, you may only be making a small fraction of what the overall profits are. If that's the case, you may be forced to work longer and harder to increase your web traffic, which may eat into your bottom line.

High Ticket Affiliate Marketing

High ticket can either be an unusually high commission or a product that sells for quite a bit of money. The payouts from high ticket products are much higher than low ticket items, but carry with them their own set of challenges.

The biggest challenge with high ticket affiliate marketing is the fact that you will not see high numbers of conversion. Higher price points will always cause consumers to hesitate, and if the price point is high, you may only see one or two sales of that product within a month. However, the good news is that even if you can sell a handful of these high ticket items a month, you will still be sitting pretty, having earned a fat commission.

To sell high ticket items, you'll need to focus less on generating traffic volume and instead focus on targeting a particular type of customer. Once you're able to create profiles of these customers and attract them via targeted marketing, you'll increase your chances of getting these conversions.

So to contrast the two, low ticket affiliate marketing focuses more on volume the more people that you can get to your site, the better. The more products you can sell, the more you will make. You may be taking less of a commission on these sales, but the volume makes up for it. On the other hand, you have high ticket affiliate marketing, which focuses more on the quality of traffic. By targeting a smaller demographic that has a higher likelihood of converting, a single sale can beat out a months worth of low ticket sales. However, the difficulty of getting that single sale is relatively high and will require persuasive copy and well put together marketing methods.

So which type is right for you? Well, that's the best part about affiliate marketing, you are free to experiment and try anything you like. Some publishers may find that they excel at selling a large volume of products, whereas others may feel more at home focusing on high-quality leads.

Regardless of the type of ticket items you are selling, it is important to remember that you will only receive back what you have invested. Affiliate marketing is easy to learn, hard to master. The ability to create a functional website that will generate sales for you requires time, energy and patience. Some people may look at high ticket items, see the amount of revenue they can pull in and think that affiliate marketing is some get rich quick scheme. That could not be further from the truth. You will not get rick quickly with affiliate marketing, regardless of how big of a ticket you are offering. Instead, by following the principles of good affiliate marketing practices, you will find that over time, your revenue will increase month after month. You may need a single sale to make a large amount of money, but the difficulty lies in getting at least one person to click on the buy button. Let's move on to the next chapter and learn what is necessary to get started with affiliate marketing.

Quiz

1. What is high ticket affiliate marketing
    a. Selling expensive products
    b. Collecting large commissions
    c. Both A and B
    d. Generating a large amount of traffic
2. Customers are more reluctant to make high-cost purchases
    a. True
    b. False
3. You cannot make money selling low ticket items
    a. True
    b. False

Chapter 3: What Do You Need For Affiliate Marketing?

The first thing that you need to get started with affiliate marketing is a professional attitude. Many times it is easy to look at online methods of gaining money as quick and easy. There can be an impatience, a desire to see results right away and when there is no evidence of fast money rolling in, the project will be abandoned.

If you want to be successful as an affiliate marketer, you must treat this endeavor as if you were starting your own business. The income potential is quite high, and there is a possibility of turning this into a full-time business. So, moving forward, you will want to treat affiliate marketing just as seriously as you would any other type of job. That is the only way that you will find true financial success in the future. If you were to treat it casually, only putting in a minimal effort, you would only receive minimal results. What you invest in terms of time and effort will pay back dividends. With that in mind, let's look at each component that you'll need to become an affiliate marketer.

A Website

The essential part of affiliate marketing is the website. The website will be the hub, the central location for all of the content that you host. The end goal is to drive as much traffic as possible to your website so that customers will be able to click on affiliate links and get you money.

Building a website today is relatively easy to do, thanks to content management systems like WordPress, that offer everything you need to make a website. You'll want to use WordPress, since you can add all sorts of valuable plugins that will aid in things such as tracking, monitoring traffic and creating banner ads.

A profitable niche

The internet is a vast place, and there is a lot of content out there. Since anyone can create a website meant to sell affiliate products, there is quite a bit of competition. A niche is an interest that is hyper-specific to a smaller group of people online. A right niche is one that is underserved by the marketplace, meaning that there aren't as many people catering to that market's needs. It opens up space for an entrepreneur to enter and sell their products to people who are actively searching for solutions to their unique problems. We'll cover how to find a niche in a later chapter.

An Organic Source of Traffic

There needs to be something that is bringing you traffic to your website. The most significant source of organic traffic is content. People flock to websites that offer excellent and interesting content for them to consume. There are many different types of content that websites offer, but they all offer value to the consumer. Without substance that is both interesting and relevant, there is no reason for a consumer to visit a website. Excellent and interesting content, on the other hand, will help generate plenty of free, organic traffic over the months.

A membership to an affiliate marketing program

When you're first starting, you'll need to have a membership with an affiliate marketing program. There are many different ways to join a program. Some advertisers offer direct programs, where you host links, whereas others require an application process, sharing details about your website before you can use their affiliate program

How hard is the application process?

In general, applying isn't hard. Advertisers want to have as many publishers as they can because each publisher provides them with marketing results. However, they also tend to be a bit discerning when it comes to picking who they work with. Some programs may want to see statistics, including page traffic and monthly visit numbers. Others may want to know what topics your website covers, and may refuse to work with you because your niche doesn't match what they are selling. Don't worry too much about being rejected from one affiliate marketing program, because there are plenty of others out there to choose from.

My application has been approved, now what?

Once your application has been successfully approved, you can now start integrating product links and banners onto your website. Most affiliates provide you the necessary connections and instructions so that you can make the most out of your time working for them.

Be advised that some affiliate programs will want to see results within a time frame. For example, Amazon Affiliates is generous with most applicant but will want to see profits within 90 days. If you aren't generating enough sales, they will shut you down and require you to reapply, to ensure that their affiliate links aren't being neglected.

Quiz

1. A website isn't necessary for successful affiliate marketing
   a. True
   b. False
2. Affiliate programs are often looking for
   a. Web traffic
   b. Sales results
   c. Credibility
   d. All of the above
3. What is most necessary to be successful in affiliate marketing?
   a. A professional attitude
   b. A nice looking website
   c. Traffic
   d. All of the above

Chapter 4: What are the Top Affiliate Marketing Programs?

With affiliate marketing being one of the most popular types of online marketing, there is no shortage of programs to choose from. We've compiled a list of the top affiliate programs and will provide short descriptions of each one.

Amazon Associates:

Amazon Associates is one of the most effective affiliates marketing programs for a variety of reasons. The biggest is that Amazon is the largest online company on the planet. People use Amazon for just about everything. If someone were to click on an Amazon affiliate link, anything they purchase through that link provides you with a commission. It means that an individual can click an Amazon link, realize they want to buy something else and make the purchase right then and there. You'll still receive the commission if that's the case.

The downside of working with Amazon Associates is that the commissions are relatively tiny compared to other programs. Offering commissions that range between 4 to 10 percent, Amazon Associates won't generate a large amount of profit for you on each sale. However, the fact that they are easy to use provides a broad array of product, and most consumers trust using them can make them extremely handy if you're starting out in the affiliate marketing world.

CJ.com

CJ Affiliate, short for Commission Junction, is an affiliate program that works with thousands of advertisers, working to connect them with publishers. With a large number of advertisers to choose from and a big infrastructure, CJ is a great affiliate program to work with. The only downside is that you'll need to apply to work with each advertiser that you do find, which takes more time and energy. This also means that you won't be guaranteed in finding an advertiser to publish for. However, CJ does make finding these advertisers easy and they have tools that make getting paid directly.

Clickbank

Clickbank is one of the largest and most generous of the affiliate programs out there. With higher than average commissions and a wide variety of products to sell, they can be a great affiliate network to work with. There are a few downsides, however. The first is that they do have a wide variety of products, and some of these products may not be of the highest quality. This means you'll need to be discerning as you select which products you want to sell on your site, as you don't want to choose low-quality products that won't move off the shelf. The other downside is that Clickbank handles refunds directly, so if a customer for some reason changes their mind and wants a refund, Clickbank will handle the refund and will almost always do so automatically. This means a portion of your sales may end up bouncing back each month, especially if the products you are selling aren't of good quality. Still, with that being said, Clickbank has a high level of potential for entrepreneurs who are willing to put in time and energy.

Rakuten Linkshare

Rakuten is one of the oldest affiliate marketing networks out there. While they don't have the most significant amount of advertisers as some of the other options on this list, they do focus much more on high-quality products to sell. In addition to the high-quality products, they have excellent tracking systems, advertising methods such as rotating banners to offer and plenty of tools and education to provide users with. One downside is that payments aren't issued consistently, as they only pay out after the merchant has been paid and that can be within 60 days of purchase. Another downside is that Rakuten is just looking for high-quality affiliates, so you'll need to demonstrate that you are worth it before they are willing to work with you. So if you're just starting out, Rakuten isn't the program for you.

JVZoo

JVZoo functions similarly to other affiliate networks, although it isn't as concerned with an application process as other affiliate programs are. Instead, you will still need to deal directly with each advertiser that is on the platform, relegating the function of JVZoo as just a middleman. However, there are no startup fees, they are relatively easy to work with, and they are growing rather quickly. This puts them in the top selection for affiliate programs to choose from. The only major downside to working with them is that they aren't as discerning about their advertisers as other networks are, so you will have to be careful in evaluating the products for sale.

AvantLink

AvantLink is a well-established affiliate program that has value for both beginners and those who have been in the affiliate marketing field for a while. They provide great features, such as automated methods of creating affiliate links for you, which will save you a lot of time. In addition, they also have great merchants and ways to vet each advertise, so you know exactly what you're getting. The downside is that AvantLink is selective when it comes to the publishers that they will work with. They only accept a small percentage of applications, so make sure that your website is up to snuff before you apply. Another common complaint about AvantLink is that they don't have the best customer support, so if you are someone who has a lot of questions about the company, you may want to aim towards a more customer service oriented program.

eBay

While eBay is famous for its online auctions, they also run their own affiliate program. This program can be quite generous, especially towards those who are able to direct users into creating brand new eBay accounts. Singing up for eBay's program is easy to do, as they are looking for as wide a net as they can cast. Their commission structures are relatively high, and since the company is well established, you won't have to worry about the credibility issue. Most people are familiar with eBay and as such, are more willing to make purchases from them.

A possible downside to eBay is the fact that the products are often used. While this might not bother a specific type of population, such as those looking for antiques, it may turn off a larger portion of the population. So really, it depends on the niche market that you are working with. If the niche is looking for previously owned products, eBay is great, but if they are looking for brand new stuff, then you may run into some trouble finding those products brand new on eBay.

Shareasale

Shareasale is a premium affiliate marketing program that has quite a bit of exclusive deals with advertisers. This means that the products they offer aren't available to other networks. So if you're looking for a way to get an edge on the competition, working with Shareasale isn't a bad idea. They offer a decent commission rate when you're starting out, but you can scale up as you perform better over time. One of the drawbacks is that the website interface isn't as intuitive as others can be, which takes time to learn. It may be a bit overwhelming at first, but if you can adapt to it, you should be able to make money with them.

Avangate

If you're looking to sell digital products and software, then Avangate is one of the best affiliate marketing programs out there. They focus primarily on selling anything digitally related, eschewing physical goods for downloadables. On top of that, they also create coupons within their affiliate network, which can boost your marketing efforts, as a coupon can help motivate a consumer to make that purchase decision. In addition to the coupon feature, they offer over 4,000 advertisers to choose from. It's basically a one-stop shop if you want to sell online products.

Maxbounty

Maxbounty is a cost-per-action affiliate and is considered to be one of the better ones out there. Offering bounties for generating not only sales but also clicks, Maxbounty is free to sign up for and offers a host of valuable tools for tracking leads. They have a significant number of advertisers, over 20,000 total, which gives you a lot to choose from. While they provide a lot of options for making money, they are discerning, which means you'll have to go through a lengthy application process with them. There's a chance you may end up being denied as well. However, if you do manage to get in, there are all sorts of incentives to work with them, such as bonuses after generating a certain number of sales a month.

Revenuewire

Revenuewire is another software focused affiliate program. They offer incredibly generous commissions, as well as a variety of different ways that you can make money. They have a wide range of software products that they sell, most of which tend to be targeted towards very specific niches. If you're looking for software sales options, then Revenuewire might be a good fit for you.

FlexOffers

Another great affiliate option, FlexOffers has over 12,000 advertisers, which dramatically increases the pool that you can select from when it comes to offering good products. They have dedicated managers who are focused on working with affiliates and provide great data metrics so you can analyze the performance of the links you are providing. One of the more significant downsides is that FlexOffers isn't so flexible when it comes to payments. They only offer direct deposit or check payouts, so if you're hoping for online services, such as PayPal, you're out of luck. Otherwise, they are a great affiliate program to work with.

PeerFly

PeerFly is another cost per action affiliate program. While they boast a smaller number of affiliates than other, larger markets, they do offer more massive payouts than most. With training tools for new users and incentives to earn a profit through contests, they aren't a bad choice, especially if you're looking to make money per click instead of per sale. However, applying for PeerFly isn't an easy process and is often lauded as being unnecessarily tricky and complicated.

Tradedoubler

Tradedoubler is a larger affiliate network that has some seriously big names attached to their brands, such as Philips, Groupo, and even Microsoft. With 2,000 advertisers and tons of tools to aid publishers with making sales, Tradedoubler is an excellent choice of an affiliate program. However, Tradedoubler is focused more on international sales, specifically the UK than any other country, which means they are looking for a significant amount of traffic coming from the UK. If you don't have those numbers, you most likely won't be able to work with them.

Chapter 5: What To Consider when Choosing an Affiliate Marketing Program

As seen in the chapter above, there are quite a few different programs that you can choose from when it comes to getting started with affiliate marketing. The real question is, how do you know which program is the right one for you? Really, it's a matter of both preference and convenience. Some affiliate programs are more open and easy to access, while others require you to demonstrate credibility by having good traffic or a certain number of sales each month. Here are a few things to keep in mind when selecting an affiliate program.

Check the advertisers

It's important not to get too excited at the idea of an affiliate program having a large number of advertisers. Sure, most programs will try to taut having several thousands of vendors to choose from, but quantity does not always equal quality. You'll want to spend time looking through your potential affiliate program's advertiser list and take a look at the products that they have to offer. Ask yourself, are these good products? Would people feel comfortable buying them? Do the websites look credible?

Credibility is an important part of the sales equation. You want advertisers that look credible to have good reviews and most importantly, have excellent websites that don't look sketchy. While you won't have to worry about credibility with certain large brands or affiliates using Amazon, it is something to consider when picking smaller advertisers. For example, if you are eying an advertiser who has a strange looking website, complete with a mix of foreign and English words present, broken links and greatly exaggerated claims, it doesn't matter if they are offering a 90% commission, getting people to buy from that store will be pretty tough. Conversely, a clean, well-cut website and sales page presented by advertisers who know the value of projecting a good image can significantly increase your chances of sales.

Don't make the mistake of thinking all advertisers are created equal; they aren't. Just because they are willing to work with you doesn't mean that they are worth it. Some advertisers, especially the ones whose products are solely digital, won't have quality goods. Due diligence is required, especially if you want to make serious money online.

Find programs with the best commission rate

You want to find programs that have the best commission rates available, that's a given. However, you may find that your options are limited since you're just beginning. High commission rates equal high competition, as more affiliate publishers will be eager to get a large slice of the pie as well. Competing with well-established niche sites will prove difficult, especially if you're both selling the same products, so you might want to hold off on going for the biggest bounties at the beginning.

The second challenge with high commissions is that most of the biggest commissions are only available to those with proven track records. This means if you're not already showing some signs of success with your marketing efforts, you most likely will have trouble getting access to these high commissions. This is only a temporary problem, of course. Once you become successful in your first endeavors, that will open up the door for more opportunity.

So while you will want to try and get the best commissions you can, don't worry too much about it when you are just starting out. Like any business, the more success you find, the more opportunities you will have to grow your business in both scale and profit. The most important thing to focus on is acquiring high-quality advertisers to sell for so that you can get those statistics that will open up the potential for higher commissions.

Consider the Quality of the Backend Services

So you found a crazy good affiliate program that offers great advertisers and high levels of commissions. That means you're done searching, right? Not necessarily. Before you take the plunge and commit to working with that affiliate program, you might want to consider what you'll be facing on the backend. Is there good customer support if you run into a problem? How often are payments made? Are the tools the affiliate program offers really useful or do they just sound good in theory?

You'll need to consider these questions and dig around to get the proper answers. Don't look to the affiliate program themselves to answer these questions, however. Of course, they will tell you that they have the best possible customer service. Instead, you'll want to find third-party reviews that can give you honest assessments of these programs, showing both the pros and the cons. Things in the affiliate marketing world are in a constant state of flux, so make sure that you are looking at the most up to date reviews as well. Remember, people have been talking about affiliate marketing for a long time, do your best to avoid articles from five years ago, the chances are that data has long since changed.

Quiz

1. When starting out, I automatically qualify for the best commission rate
   a. True
   b. False
2. What qualities does a good advertiser have?
   a. Good products
   b. Well designed websites
   c. Low prices
   d. Both A and B
3. How can you determine if an affiliate program is trustworthy?
   a. Check their own website
   b. Look to third-party reviews
   c. Trust your gut
   d. Just try it and see if it works out

Chapter 6: How to Create Content for Affiliate Marketing

If you want to be a successful affiliate marketer, you need to be a successful content creator. As the adage goes, content is king. Content is the reason that people will visit your website, it is the reason they will return, and it is the reason that they will recommend your site to others. If you want to succeed, you're going to need to learn the fundamental principles of what makes for great content.

What is Content?

At its core, content can be considered anything that provides value to potential customers. A well-written blog post is content. A funny video is content. A product review is content. The purpose of content is to provide some kind of value to a consumer, either through educating them, entertaining them or inspiring them. Customers browse websites entirely for the purpose of consuming good content. They're looking for articles and videos that provide them with value and in return, create connections with the content providers who offer such things.

As an affiliate marketer, you're going to want to produce content that is relevant to your target audience. For example, if you are providing fisher gear affiliate links, you'll want to create content that solely targets people who would be interested in fishing. This means creating blog pages talking about fishing techniques, making videos reviewing fishing products that are on the market, and developing other types of content that would appeal to those who fish.

By creating relevant content that provides value to consumers, you are creating organic sources of traffic to your website. This allows you to passively generate sales without having to spend any money on advertising costs.

One of the challenges behind creating content for the sake of affiliate marketing is that you will most definitely want to include your links into these articles. However, your primary goal should be to provide value to the reader, not to make sales. While this may seem counterintuitive, you have to realize that affiliate marketing is about creating good relationships with customers. If you create low-quality content that only pushes readers to buy your products, this will be met with frustration on the consumer's end. They will most likely disengage from your website and not visit again.

On the flipside, if you are able to generate high-quality content that serves a need in the reader's life, then they will begin to regard you as an authority on the matter. Even more so, they will return to your website, time and time again. So if they don't convert the first time they visit, there is still hope that at some point, they will make a conversion. On top of that, they may share your content with others, which widens your net even more.

Relationship is the heart of content creation. The goal is to build a good, healthy relationship with those who visit your website. Sales come later, once that trust has been established. If you do a good job and build a strong relationship, you may find that customers will begin looking to you solely for making their consumer decisions about the niche you are in. If that's the case, you will be looking at long term sales with that consumer.

Promoting Products You Have Used

One of the easiest types of content to produce is product reviews. Consumers are always on the hunt for good reviews, and if the niche you are working in is narrow, that means there might not be a lot of reviews available. Product reviews are inherently valuable because the people who are reading those reviews are looking to make a purchase. If you review effectively, you could very well see a conversion by the time the consumer has finished reading or watching your review.

Of course, creating reviews takes time and understanding of the product. The best type of product reviews are the ones that show the creator has inside knowledge of the product and has used it in action. Having access to the product and using it yourself will go a long way in creating credibility. It will also provide you with a hands-on understanding of the product, which will naturally help you understand what to talk about.

What medium should you use for a review? It depends on the product and the level of energy you want to put into it. Written reviews work fine for most products, but if a product has a demonstratable effect, you might want to consider creating a video review. It doesn't have to be anything fancy, and most folks can get away with just using their phone cameras to make video reviews these days.

You should strive for both honesty and accuracy when writing these reviews. The more a reader can come to rely upon you, the more they will expect for you to show that you have an understanding of these products. If you document features that don't exist, lie about results or otherwise exaggerate, just in the hopes of making a sale, it will damage your credibility. In the world of online marketing, credibility is the one resource that you simply cannot purchase. Don't make the mistake of short-term thinking. A single sale isn't nearly as valuable as multiple sales from the same consumers, year after year. You will only get those sales when the consumer trusts you, and that requires for you to post honest reviews.

Presenting Products You Haven't Used

Realistically, you aren't going to have used every single product that you are selling online. Either the products don't have any value for you, or the price range puts them outside of your budget. Either way, this isn't too much of problem, as long as you tackle it head-on. Instead of trying to present as if you are an authority on these products, just spend the time and effort doing all the research that a consumer would do. Most people are looking to save time, so if you are able to compile a list of reviews and documented third parties who speak favorably about the product, you can still vouch for the product without having used it yourself. Sure, you won't be able to say "I personally approve this product," but then again, if you have a significant amount of research that says the product is good, most consumers won't care.

All you need to focus on is compiling accurate and valuable research. Placing all of these facts into one area, so that your readers are able to look through them quickly and efficiently can be extremely helpful. Your role in the case of products you haven't reviewed personally is that of a research assistant. You want to help educate your customers, looking at your web space as a centralized place to share these reviews. This can help move customers from the questioning phase to the purchase phase rather quickly, especially if they are looking for good reasons to buy.

Just like with your own personal reviews, make sure that you are honest and open about these products. If you find shortcomings, don't hide them away, instead display them honestly and earnestly. You want customers to be as informed as possible. It's rare for a product to be absolutely perfect and a customer is looking at only good reviews will quickly grow suspect. Throwing a few honest, fair and even-handed negative aspects about the product is a great way to build trust and give the customer a decent picture of what you are selling.

What Type of Content Should I Create?

Since content creation is one of the most important aspects of affiliate marketing, you should be prepared to spend the most substantial amount of time possible on creating a content schedule. A content schedule will allow you to plan ahead, figuring out exactly what types of content that you will publish and when.

There are really three core types of content that can be made: content that entertains, content that educates and content that inspires. These three types are quite broad and cover a wide array of subcategories. But in general, you either want to encourage people, educate them or make them happy through entertainment.

There are many ways to create content, from making videos to writing articles and even to creating infographics that help consumers learn interesting facts about the niche. The most important thing to remember is that content should exist purely for the sake of adding something useful to the lives of your customer. Sure, you can include affiliate links in some of the content that you create, and you can run banner ads selling your products on any of your pages, but at the end of the day, you must be willing to add something to a customer's life for free.

Content should only be relevant to your niche as well. You don't want to attract a broad audience, because a general audience won't convert as quickly as a targeted one. Therefore, it is essential to focus on only creating content that is relevant to your niche in some way. The more targeted traffic you can generate with your content, the bigger chance you have of making sales in some way.

Another thing to keep in mind is that you want to create what's known as Evergreen content. Evergreen means timeless. Whether it's six months in the future or six years, a piece of Evergreen content remains relevant no matter the passage of time. This will aid you greatly, as you will be able to reuse your content from time to time, either reposting the blog post or promoting it on social media. Plus, when you have readers first make contact with their website, they will find reward in going through your backlogs, as the content will remain relevant to them, despite the year that you posted it.

Blog posts are the most common types of content that a website can generate. These posts contain one of the three different content subjects, entertain, educate or inspire. You will want to create a decent amount of blog posts and then keep updating it week to week, that way you can be sure that readers are regularly returning to your site. You should sit and work to create different categories of posts that you want to be producing in the long term. Product reviews, previews, helpful hints in the niche field or humorous discussions are all excellent subjects to write about.

On top of blog posts, if possible, you should work to make visual content as well. Whether it be a few infographics, a demonstration video or a humorous illustration, the visual medium is often shared to friends and family. This can help generate leads organically and in the process, increase the chances of getting someone to make repeat visits to your website.

How Much Content Should I Make?

When you're first getting started, you will want to try and create as much content as possible, enough so that it takes a reader more than one sitting to go through the entire backlog. This will help establish your website as an authority on the niche you have select and in the process, solidify your relationship with readers. Once you have a large backlog of content created, you can then adjust the schedule of when you release content. At the least, you'll want to focus on releasing content at least once a week. If possible, you may want to increase the frequency of new content to at least three times a week. The more content you release, the more readers will visit your site to look at what's new. And the more they read, the higher the chances of getting a conversion!

I'm not a writer/content creator. What do I do?

If you don't have the skill for writing, don't panic! You don't have to be a brilliant author to generate useful content. Instead, you'll need to hire freelancers to create content for you. This will cost you some money in the short term, so only do it if you are confident that you will see a return from your investment. If you aren't fully committed to your website or niche, the last thing you want to do is waste your money on content that won't generate you any sales.

Hiring a content creator is relatively simple. you'll just want to use a freelancer website such as

Upwork and look for writers who fit your price point. Then just give them the topics you want them to write on and wait for them to finish up. If you have the budget for it, you can generate quite a bit of article a month this way. The best part is that if you start getting sales from your efforts, you can reinvest and continue to see more content generated by these freelancers.

Create A Podcast

One of the most definitive ways you can position yourself as an authority figure in a niche is to develop a podcast. Long-form audio content is one of the most rapidly growing industries right now, and advertisers are starting to pick up on it. The fact is, people who listen to podcasts often feel that they have a connection to the show hosts and as such, are willing to trust the words of the host.

While guest starring on a podcast can be useful for a short-term spike in your website traffic and even sales, running your own podcast would be even better. All you really need to get started is a decent microphone and a format for your show. Since you already have your niche figured out, you won't have to worry about picking a topic for your show either, as it will already be in your chosen field.

The important thing to remember about a good podcast is that its purpose is to build a better connection with your audience. You are also free to pitch products as much as you like, as most people understand that podcasts need sponsors. These two factors combined means that podcasts are one of the most powerful types of content that you can have in your pocket.

You may be intimidated by the idea of running a podcast, but in reality, it's not too hard to do. Some basic editing skills, such as learning how to cut out the pauses, uhms and ahs, a good topic of discussion and a few guests on your show will do wonders. Plus, as you build a fanbase, you may end up attracting more listeners, and you could even end up selling ad space to sponsors. The benefits of running a podcast are incredibly high and to be honest, there aren't any drawbacks. The worst case scenario is that you make a few shows and nobody listens. The best case scenario is that you are able to establish yourself as persuasive authority in your niche and directly market to listeners.

Consistency is key

Above all, when it comes to content creation, you'll want to be as consistent with your release schedule as possible. Pick a specific day of the week and commit to releasing content on that day. This will help condition your readers to visit you on those days. If you miss a week, they might grow disappointed, and if you lose two or three, they very well may stop visiting you actively. No matter what, even if the blog post isn't crazy long, hit your schedule every week. You don't want to lose readers week to week.

Quiz

1. What are the three primary types of content?
    a. Education, Inspiration, and Entertainment
    b. Infographics, Videos and Blog Posts
    c. Facebook, Instagram, and Twitter
    d. Education, Entertainment, and Information
2. Consistency is unimportant when it comes to content scheduling
    a. True
    b. False
3. If you aren't good at writing, you should
    a. Give up
    b. Hire a writer
    c. Steal other content and repackage it as your own
    d. Both A and C
4. Why is content so important?
    a. It drives traffic to your website
    b. It establishes authority on a niche
    c. It has the potential for generating sales
    d. All of the Above

Chapter 7: How to utilize social media platforms for Affiliate Marketing

Social media is one of the most important tools when it comes to making sales online. Social media will allow for users to share your content with each other, which ultimately directs them to your home page. From there, a curious reader will begin to poke around and may end up coming across a product that they like. If that's the case, you could make a conversion without even paying a cent for that traffic!

If you want to be successful as an affiliate marketer then you just *cannot* ignore social media. The value of the platforms is just too high to leave alone. At the same time, social media can be tricky to master. Many marketers look at it as simply an avenue for free advertising and in the process, make a ton of mistakes that hurt their image and cost them time and energy. If you want to be successful with social media as an affiliate marketer, you need to approach it with a level of caution. Don't just throw yourself into the fray. instead, develop a strategy and stick to it. Let's look at some ways that you can increase your social media results.

Find the Platform that your target market is using

Not all social media platforms are the same. There is a big difference between how Facebook, Twitter and Instagram function. On top of that, each platform is suited for a different type of user experience. Some niches thrive on Twitter, whereas other niches are heavily invested in using Facebook groups to discuss what they like. You'll need to spend some time researching these platforms and look to see which platform your niche works with the most. You don't have to use every single social media platform out there to be successful. Instead, you just have to find the ones that have the highest concentration of your target market. For example, if you're aiming for a younger audience, then you'll most likely want to target Instagram, which traditionally has a younger demographic than Facebook. If the products you are selling are for writers, then Twitter would be the ideal platform to use, as the open discussion leads a lot of people to have conversations with each other. Do the research and figure out where your target market tends to crowd together the most. Then, make that your primary platform for marketing.

Identify Which Content to Share on Each Platform

Every platform has different styles, and that means different types of content thrive in different social networks. For example, Instagram is almost purely based on visual content, while Facebook thrives with a mix of visual and written content. This shouldn't take too much of your time, but spend some effort learning which types of content perform the best on each platform. That way, when you plan your social media sharing, you will be able to identify which platform to upload your content to.

Find out how content is spread in a network

One important thing to learn is how content moves through social networks. For example, Twitter has a retweet function, that allows people to report a tweet, sharing it with their friends. Instagram, however, has no such purpose and only has the ability to like pictures. Spend some time studying how different types of content are spread through your chosen social media platform, so you know what to expect when you share your own content.

Don't overshare your content

At the end of the day, whenever you share your content on social media, the end goal is to see an uptick in website traffic and hopefully a few conversions. This can narrow your vision and cause you to treat social media like it's nothing more than a traffic generating machine. However, this isn't the case. First off, most social media platforms have their own ad systems and systems that they want you to pay for. They often have algorithmic restrictions that prevent repeated content posts from spreading too far out, even if you have a large number of followers. For example, Facebook only lets one post a day have the highest amount of organic reach. Any more posts than just the one and you will quickly find that you will have diminishing results. This is because Facebook sells its own ads and want you to purchase ad space from them. They don't want you to use their platform entirely for free.

So it's important to know that the results you see from organic posting will be limited. So don't waste too much of your time oversharing. Find out what the ideal posting schedule is for each platform that you are using and stick that schedule. Don't try to go past that, because you will only see diminishing results.

Build Connections and relationships

Social media is just that *social!* While you might be a business, it's still important to recognize that personal relationships are one of the most important parts of creating a connection with customers. Don't just look at social media as an opportunity to push your products and your content. Instead, look at it as an opportunity to create a dialogue with your readers, make connections with them and most importantly, learn what they want. When you are able to listen and learn from your readers through social media, you can adapt on the fly to improve your content. Taking suggestions will sharpen your website's appeal and as such, increase your sales and readership.

Conversely, if you only focus on pushing your own content through social media, most people will come to recognize you as nothing more than a shill. Nobody likes to be sold without permission. If they see someone constantly spamming away, talking only about themselves, they will quickly be turned off. This will cut off the relationship and in the end, will just sabotage your efforts.

A good marketer knows that friendship and connection will help increase both credibility and sales in the future. So don't just treat your followers and fans on social media as nothing more than pieces of data. Talk to them. Ask them questions. Learn about their wants and desires. Share content that isn't yours; share ideas that are relevant and meaningful. Create real connections and grow your business in both authority and credibility!

Use Facebook and LinkedIn Groups

Facebook and LinkedIn both have special functions known as groups. These groups are often private clubs where members can connect and talk with each other about specific topics. Anyone can create a Facebook group and invite members as they please. Some groups are open to anyone to join, but you should exhibit caution when interacting with these groups. The last thing they want is for someone to join their community and start marketing straight to them.

Instead, you should create your own group, allowing for people interested in your product and content to join up. This will create a small community where you can answer questions, offer solutions and share more of your unique content with them. If the community begins to grow, that's even better, because you may have your members inviting others to join. Over time, you may find yourself with a small, targeted group full of people who are interested in your content and products. This will open up many possibilities for direct sales.

Quiz

1. Social media is best for
   a. Creating relationships with fans and followers
   b. Selling products constantly
   c. Sharing content
   d. Both A and C
2. The best platform to use is
   a. Facebook
   b. Twitter
   c. Snapchat
   d. The platform your target demographic uses the most
3. People want to be sold to when using social media
   a. True
   b. False

Chapter 8: What are the common Affiliate Marketing Pitfalls?

Affiliate marketing has a relatively low barrier to entry, which means most people can get involved with it if they like. However, just because there isn't anything keeping you from getting started with affiliate marketing doesn't mean that it's easy. In fact, becoming successful in affiliate marketing can be somewhat hard in the beginning. There are so many simple mistakes that can be made that hurt you both in time and even in money. These mistakes can lead to discouragement or worse, just giving up! Let's take a look at some of the most common pitfalls of affiliate marketing and the ways that you can overcome them.

Refusing to spend money

Let's face it. You don't need a lot of money to get started with affiliate marketing. There aren't a crazy amount of fees involved at the beginning. While there are some affiliate programs that charge for membership, you can always find other affiliates that offer their services for free. The most significant cost that you may incur is the cost of creating the website, making content and buying the domain name.

However, just because you can shoestring an affiliate marketing operation doesn't mean that you should avoid spending money no matter what. There are certain things that you should be willing to pay your money on, things such as advertising, membership fees, and content design. These things are all designed to help you make more money in the future. Advertising will especially be one of your most significant costs as you work to expand your business size.

Some new affiliate marketers may get in the habit of refusing to spend money. They look at the prospect of spending a few bucks here and there as a bad thing, expecting only to see returns from their efforts. But the problem here is that you're running a business. Very few businesses can be created and sustained for free. Instead of fretting about money as if it will never be seen again, a good affiliate marketing realizes that they are investing their dollars. Investments are meant to bring about returns, and with affiliate marketing, the returns can be tremendous. Yes, there will be costs you incur as you go along, but the costs are significantly lower than running any other kind of traditional business.

Spending Too Much Money

Another problem that can plague beginners is the urge to spend too much money when getting started. There are plenty of programs, courses, guides and other types of resources out there that promise all sorts of great results. All you need to do is buy X program, and it'll do all of the heavy liftings, or so the ad claims. The problem with a lot of these programs isn't necessarily that they don't' work, but rather inexperienced affiliate marketer's don't have the experience to use them to their full potential.

When you're just getting started, you should sit down and create a realistic budget for your first affiliate marketing website. This budget should include everything that you need to get the website up and running. This includes content creation, web design costs, hosting, domain name, and your initial advertising budget. Spend some time analyzing how much it's going to cost, run the numbers and come up with a proper budget. Then, stick to it. Don't give in to the urge to spend too much on any of these things, as you are just starting out. More importantly, don't go outside of your budget to purchase "necessary" software and programs until you have already proven to yourself that you can make money without them.

Don't fall into the trap of spending way too much at the beginning. First off, you don't even know if your niche is going to be profitable. If you put too much money into a project at the beginning and it turns out to be a bust, you've just lost a significant amount of investment. Instead, spend your money in phases, increasing your spending only as you see results.

Not Building a Community from Day One

Community is one of the most valuable pieces behind affiliate marketing. When you decide that you want to create a website, you are doing more than just putting up some words on a Wordpress theme. You're building a brand and an identity. A community is one of those things that will help reinforce and grow your brand over time. Some marketers ignore the community aspect and only focus on themselves, working to create one-sided websites that don't tap into the vast number of people who visit on a daily basis. But this is a tremendous mistake. A community allows for likeminded people to gather around your website and discuss things with each other. It allows for them to ask you the important questions and certain members may even be able to answer those questions for you. A community will naturally help increase the size and loyalty of your following.

Creating a community isn't difficult to do either. Some opt to create forums on their website, where like-minded individuals can gather together to talk about your chosen niche. Others only work to create Facebook groups or Twitter pages where discussions can be held. There are many different ways for you to create and foster a community as a marketer. If you get started on day one, your community will grow right along with your website. The more the people that decide to join your community, the more significant impact they will have on others within their circles. Don't ignore the power of a community; instead, do everything that you can to harness it.

Becoming too salesy by exaggerating results

Your credibility is one of the most important things when it comes to online marketing. People aren't going to trust you much when they first meet you online. The nature of the internet can be predatory, and people need to be cautious when dealing with any new source of information. Over time, when you display things that make you trustworthy, people will begin to warm up to you. Credibility is hard to earn but incredibly easy to lose. All you need to do is make a single misstep, and you could potentially destroy a year's worth of trust.

Many new affiliate marketers look at the bottom line as the only thing that matters. Their eyes get too wide at the idea of getting a sale, and they become tempted to make shortcuts. One such alternative is exaggerating the results and value of a product. A product isn't simply helpful, no, they claim that is the last product that you will ever need to buy in this niche. It will solve all of the customer's problems. It will last forever. It's virtually indestructible. The list goes on and on, but the end results are always the same. The consumer makes the purchase, realizes that they've been had and they lose all trust in you. Sure, you landed a sweet $20.00 commission, but you lost a customer for the rest of your life.

At the end of the day, all you have is your credibility. Protect it with your life. Don't exaggerate, don't lie and certainly don't take moral shortcuts. A sale is once, but a reputation is forever.

Not Working With a Partner

While it is true that you can go it alone when working as an affiliate marketer, working alone can be somewhat overwhelming. There are so many moving parts to a good affiliate website, from creating content to analyzing metrics, to running the social media. It can be quite overwhelming over time, and you may end up suffering from a deficiency in your productivity. If that's the case, then you could be losing money!

Working with a partner is a great way to remedy these problems. By splitting the workload evenly, you will be able to maintain your website regularly without running yourself ragged. More importantly, with the right partner, you will be able to increase your profit potential. Of course, your partner won't work for free, either you'll need to pay them or offer them a proper split of the profits, but the more hands that are involved with the project, the more money you'll make.

Shiny Object Syndrome

Shiny Object Syndrome is a deadly disease that can kill a lot of entrepreneurs without them realizing it! What is it exactly? It's where an entrepreneur is continually being distracted by new business ideas or techniques. They bounce from idea to idea, never settling down and focusing on what really matters. Instead, they keep studying new technologies, keep purchasing courses, spend all of their time reading books about new types of sales methods without ever sticking with a single plan. They are perpetually in the planning phase.

Worse, if they are somehow able to get out of the planning stage and launch a website, they won't stick around for too long. They'll grow impatient with the lack of results or become fascinated with a new idea and then go about trying something entirely new, leaving behind their old endeavors.

Shiny Object Syndrome can happen to any entrepreneur who is undisciplined. Part of being a good businessperson is having the discipline to stay the course. Once you have developed a business plan, once you've done the research and all that's left is putting in the effort, you need to keep at it until you get the results your looking for. The ability to say "no" to any new idea until you have already made money on your current approach can be difficult for some people. But it what separates the wheat from the chaff. Anyone can come up with a business plan, and anyone can quickly put together a website for affiliate marketing. But what makes a true entrepreneur is the ability to stick with what you've planned to do.

Not Delegating Tasks

As hard as it may be to accept, you aren't going to be good at everything. Everyone has their strong suits and their weak areas. A good entrepreneur isn't someone who lacks weakness. Instead, it's someone who is keenly aware of their shortcomings and works to circumvent them. Suppose that you are excellent at creating websites and finding good advertisers to work with, but you struggle greatly with social media. Rather than continue to struggle, you could opt instead to hire someone to work as a social media manager, even if it's only for a few hours a month, just to help circulate your content.

It can be challenging to give up on full control of your business, especially if you're someone who has a strong need to be in charge at all times. However, by hiring out talent who can fill in the gaps, you will be increasing your potential for sales, which in turn equals higher levels of profit. It may cost you a bit of money in the short term. Everything has a trade-off. If you aren't a skilled content creator, then your website won't be competitive in the online information market. This will cause you to lag behind and in turn, will hurt your bottom line. You're always paying for something one way or another. The trick is to learn how to pay only for the things that will make you more money in the future.

Failing to track results

One of the most important parts of being an entrepreneur is learning how to follow results. You will never be able to determine if your efforts are actually working if you are unsure of any of the data. Thanks to websites like Google Analytics and Facebook Ads, we are in a golden era of information tracking. If you put in the fair amount of time required at the beginning, you'll be able to determine how many people visit your website, where the traffic is coming from, which products people are clicking on the most and other important details.

Measuring results will allow you to improve your product sales methods. You will be able to see which products are being clicked the most as well as which ones aren't being interacted with at all. With advanced result tracking systems, like heatmaps, you'll even be able to see where your readers are spending the most amount of time on your website.

The fact of the matter is that you can learn a lot about your readers and their habits, as well as how you can improve your sale pitches with analytics. However, if you fail to track them, if you neglect to learn how to analyze and interpret data, you won't have any such edge. Instead, you'll just be guessing each week when it comes to how well your website is performing. It would be akin to operating a car without ever looking at the fuel gauge. You would have no idea how much gas you have in the tank until you make the decision to look down at it. Metrics are the fuel for a good website. Check them as often as you can!

Quiz

1. How important are analytics for your business?
   a. Extremely important
   b. Moderately important
   c. Somewhat important
   d. Not important at all
2. Exaggeration is perfectly fine when it comes to marketing
   a. True
   b. False
3. Shiny Object Syndrom means
   a. Constantly getting distracted by new ideas
   b. Wanting to make more money online
   c. Fascination with mirrors
   d. Learning new methods of marketing
4. The best way to work as an affiliate marketer is alone
   a. True
   b. False

Chapter 9: How to Choose Your Niche

Picking a niche is one of the core challenges behind affiliate marketing. You'll want to find a niche that is underrepresented online, with low amounts of competition and high numbers of people interested. This is a difficult task and will take a lot of time and research. Even with the most study, there is still no guarantee that the niche you pick will perform well until you actually get the website up and running. Still, there are ways to help increase your chances for success the first time around, let's look at a few critically important steps.

Make a list of your hobbies, interests, and passions

Believe it or not, but the first step in finding a niche is to look within. Since you're going to be the one who is working on generating excellent and relevant content, you'll want to choose a niche that you are familiar with. By creating a list of your hobbies, interests, and passions, you'll be able to see if there is anything that sticks out to you. The more excited you are about a specific niche, the better chances you have of success. And the best way to get passionate about a niche is to find one that you are already interested in. The internet is a vast place, so there is a pretty big chance that there are other people who are just as excited about these hobbies or passions as you are.

Arrange the topics you've chosen in order of how much you enjoy talking about them

Once you have finished creating the lists, it's time to organize them. Put the topics that you enjoy talking about the most at the top of the list and rank them accordingly. Remember, in the beginning, you'll want to be creating a good portion of the content, and that means you will mainly be about the niche a lot. By choosing a field that you absolutely love talking about, it means you won't burn out quickly.

Survey other people's interests in the subject

Once you have a general idea of the top three or four niches that you've drawn from your list, it's time to begin looking to see if there is a wide enough interest in the subject online. This will take some time, but it is a vital part of the research phase. Search online, use tools such as Google Trends to see how many people are searching for terms that are specific to your niche. If you see that there is a wide enough market, a big enough demand for that niche, then you might have found your winner. But you're not done yet. A niche market is a combination of a narrow, specific topic and an underserved market. This means that you cannot have a substantial amount of competition if you are going to market effectively.

Survey the competition

Once you have finalized on a niche topic, you'll need to survey the competition. Look up their niche sites and make some observations. Are the websites strong? Are they well designed? Do they look like they are doing the right amount of business? Are there areas that are weak? Can you compete with them? Most importantly, is the front page of the Google search crowded with a massive competition? One or two well-designed competitors are excellent, but if you realize that every single link on the front page belongs to a different competitor with a well-designed website and a serious amount of good content, you'll definitely need to find another niche.

A niche market just cannot be too crowded with good content creators, especially if the advertiser pool for that niche is rather shallow. This may result in some disappointment, especially if you find out that your favorite topic is overcrowded, but don't worry. There are other niches to cover, or you can work to find a solution that other competitors aren't providing in this field.

Find the most commonly searched problems about this niche

By using search engine tools, such as Google Keyword Planner, you have the ability to discover what people are typing about in relation to your niche. With some time, you can look for common phrases typed about problems related to your chosen niche. For example, if you're running a fishing website, you might find that people are consistently searching for "quickly untangle reel." Then, you simply document these problems that people are encountering and move onto the next step.

Find affiliate products that can solve these problems

All marketing is really about solving problems. People have issues in their niche field and are looking for solutions. By learning what these problems are, you can then go about acquiring the solutions. Once you have found affiliate products that will solve these problems, most of the legwork is done. All you need to do is just help your readers become aware of these solutions, and those who are looking for these solutions will make the purchases as quickly as they can.

This is how you separate yourself from a niche that may have strong competitors as well. If you see a niche that has low competition, but they have sleek websites and high content, you can work to identify which problems they aren't addressing. This can give you a significant edge against them, as you can then work to obtain those solution products and then heavily incorporate them into your marketing techniques.

Quiz

1. What is the best subject for a niche?
    a. Whatever is selling
    b. A passion, interest or hobby that you love
    c. Fishing gear
    d. All of the above
2. Why is passion important when it comes to choosing a niche?
    a. You will genuinely enjoy what you are doing
    b. You will understand more about the products you are selling
    c. You will have a better level of communication with customers
    d. All of the above
3. An underserved market means
    a. There isn't a wide amount of options for consumers in that niche
    b. There is a low level of competition in the field
    c. Both A and B
    d. There is too much competition to break into
4. People purchase products because they have a problem they need solving
    a. True
    b. False

Chapter 10: How to build your email list

The email list is one of the most important parts of online marketing. An email list allows you to capture the emails of potential leads and then directly send them special offers and other types of communications. While other types of marketing efforts, such as paid ads, can quickly be ignored in passing by a consumer, email ads tend to be a little different. Since they arrive directly inside of a customer's inbox, they have a bigger chance of being read. Not only that, since the email is sent to your target demographic, you have a higher chance of conversion from them as well. This means that they might be interested in purchasing your products that your email is talking about. And the best part is that you can email the customers on your list for as often as you like, at no charge!

If you want to be a serious affiliate marketer, then you're going to have to put in the time and effort to build an effective email list. Fortunately, doing so is free and easy! Let's take a look at how you can create your email list.

Create A Lead Capture Page

The first and most crucial part of building a mailing list is to create a lead capture page. Also known as a squeeze page, this is where you will direct web traffic explicitly for the purpose of capturing emails. Emails are extremely valuable in the marketing business, so that means you should prioritize getting a hold of them as much as you can, especially when you are just starting out. A good portion of your marketing efforts should be to capture leads. This means you'll need to create a useful lead capture page.

Creating one isn't too hard. You can either simply just make one on your own website, spending some time building a different visual design to help set it apart from your regular web pages, or you can use a specific service, such as LeadPages, which offer the ability to create high functioning lead pages in a matter of minutes.

Create a unique value proposition

Part of creating a lead capture system is learning how to acquire emails. Most people will not just hand out their emails for nothing. In order to gain these emails, you'll need to offer a value proposition, offering the potential lead something in exchange for their email. These offerings are referred to as lead magnets. This can be as simple as a free eBook or perhaps even a few coupons for one of the affiliate programs that you are using. The more attractive the offer, the better chance you have of getting your lead's email address.

A good value proposition is something that is specific to the niche of your target market. You will want to offer something that is both relevant and unique to your field, offering them something that would motivate them to sign up on your email form. It doesn't have to be a wildly expensive gift either. It just needs to be something that would make your target market give pause and think "I want that." If you can get them to want your lead magnet, they will convert and give you their emails.

You want to be cautious when initially creating your lead magnet. If you build too attractive a magnet, you may end up getting leads that are low quality. These are leads that aren't super interested in your niche or what you have to sell. Instead, the only reason they signed up was for the free gift. This can happen quite often, especially if your gift is too attractive to the general public.

Instead, you should work to create something that only appeals to your core audience. Don't make the gift overwhelmingly valuable and certainly make sure that the gift will in some way move your lead closer to making a purchase.

Ask for emails in a natural way

While you will want to create a landing page that extols the virtue of joining your mailing list, you will also want to advertise for your email list on your regular website. Perhaps it'll simply be a small paragraph at the end of a blog post, or maybe it will be somewhere on the home page. Either way, if that's the case, you will want to ask for their email in a natural way. Just mention that you have a newsletter and that you'd love to send them both updates and special deals. Don't push hard. After all, people aren't directly visiting your website for an upsell. That's what the point of your landing page will be. Instead, just keep a simple reminder present, naturally asking for emails without any kind of hard sell.

Limit the number of times you ask for an email

This is one tip that most online marketers tend to forget or outright ignore. Getting an email has a lot of value, that cannot be denied, but not everyone wants to give their email away. If the value proposition isn't enough to motivate the reader to sign up, and if they have no interest in a newsletter or receiving product information, you most likely won't see a conversion from them. That's fine, but if you push too hard and too often, you may end up irritating them.

Pop-ups are a useful tool when it comes to generating emails. While most people do regard pop-up ads as an annoyance, using a well designed, inoffensive pop-up banner to show that you have a mailing list can actually a percentage of your visitors. However, you will want to make sure that you configure the pop-ups only to show themselves to new visitors. After that, make sure that your pop-ups aren't bothering the same visitors over and over again. Also, make sure that your ads don't follow them from page to page. Nothing can be more irritating than going from one link to another on a website, only to be followed by the same type of pop-up each time.

Create Many Types of Lists

You don't have to stick to just one type of email list. In fact, you really shouldn't limit yourself with just the one. Instead, you should create a few different kinds of email lists, each with different value propositions and purposes. For example, you could have a newsletter mailing list, a mailing list for sending special offers and another mailing list for referral links. Separating your leads will help you keep track of which ones are looking actively to make purchases, which ones are really just interested in the blog and which ones are open to special offers. Feel free to experiment with as many different list types as you like, until you finally have the ideal ratio that you are looking for.

Engaging with the Customer

Once you have access to the customer's emails, you are perfectly free to send them communications whenever you like. However, it is important to remember that when a customer gives you an email, it is a sign of trust. They are looking for you to provide them with some sort of value. You must treat their emails with respect and refrain from sending them too many emails a day. Instead, try to use your email list as the ability to engage with customers on a deeper level.

For example, you can use your newsletter mailing list as an opportunity to share news about your website as it grows. If you have gotten new products to review, you can talk about that, or you can share what has been going on behind the scenes. Mostly, you want to engage with your readers by giving them personal communications. This will create the picture that you are more than just some faceless website and will establish a stronger connection.

On top of that, you can also use your mailing list as an opportunity to send questions and surveys to your readers, getting a better sense of what they want to see more of on your website. This has a dual benefit, the first being that your customers get to feel that you listen and care about their opinion and the second is that you can better customize your website to meet consumer needs.

Keep Emails Confidential

One of the most important things to remember is that an email must remain confidential. When a customer entrusts you with their email, they are under the impression that you intend to use their email only for your own business purposes. This means that you must refrain from any unethical behavior, such as selling their data to other businesses.

In addition to refraining from selling their personal data, you must also make sure that you don't cross-contaminate your emails. For example, if you are running two separate websites, one selling fishing gear and the other selling hiking gear, both under two different brands, then you must treat the email lists as separate. There can be a temptation to cross-email, opting to send a few of your fishing themed emails to the hiking mailing list, but this will only cause trouble for a number of reasons.

The first reason is that a customer did not opt to sign up for the fishing mailing list, they chose into the hiking list. When they receive a fishing list, they will be confused as to why they are receiving it. The message will not be well received and most likely deleted immediately.

The second problem is that the customer might realize that they are being mailed by the same company under a different brand. This has the potential to irritate them or cause them to lose their trust in you, as they specifically wanted communication for one brand. This generates bad will which can ultimately lead to the loss of confidence or worse, the loss of a customer.

It is essential for you always to remember to keep all of your mailing lists separate from each other, out of respect for your customer. Keep their data confidential and never cross-contaminate.

Create Your Autoresponders

One great feature of using a mailing list management system such as MailChimp is the fact that they allow for automation. Autoresponders allow for you to reply specific actions, such as a sign-up, automatically, sending a premade email to your customer. So if you are offering a free eBook, for example, you will want to use an autoresponder email that will automatically send the download link to any new customer. This saves you the valuable time of having to do it yourself, and more importantly, gives a customer a great experience because they get the item of value almost instantly!

You can also use autoresponders for all manner of tasks. For example, if you want to send a personalized type of email, thanking a person for joining, a week after they get their free gift, just to remind them about your website, you can customize an autoresponder to do that. You can also use the autoresponder to send your most popular blog posts in a series, giving your reader some valuable information, arriving straight into their inbox!

But like all things pertaining to email, make sure that you don't overdo it. The last thing you want to do is accidentally flood your potential customer with too many emails in a short amount of time. Make sure that your autoresponders are spaced apart evenly and there are at least a few days in between each automatic email. Otherwise, you might risk them clicking the unsubscribe button!

Choose your email marketing approach

There are many different approaches you can take with email marketing. You can focus on a long term email campaign, meant to see conversions over a steady amount of time or you can focus on short-term blitzes, sending only a few emails to a client, but each email contains a harder sell. The choice is really up to you. But when to the approach, you'll need to consider both content and frequency.

As a rule of thumb, if the content is meant to result in a direct sale, you should send it infrequently.

Sending one or two direct sales methods within a month would be an excellent way to get started. Then, you can log those who convert and add their emails to a specific list, since they have a proven track record of being the ones who convert.

If the content isn't directly meant to sell, you can settle for a weekly email without too much fear. Creating a content schedule for your emails will help you plan out which ones you want to send and to who.

Aggressive approaches are fine, as long as you keep enough time between emails. Finding that sweet spot can be difficult, but fortunately, you have the power of metrics to evaluate your performance. If you see that sending three direct sale emails in a month results in a 60 percent loss of subscribers, you should either change your mailing frequency, improve the value of your email proposition or better yet, find higher quality subscribers. If you find that you aren't losing a lot of subscribers with your current frequency, or that you are experiencing an even higher number of conversions, then you most likely have found the perfect email frequency. Keep that up until things begin to change.

Email ad campaigns aren't an exact science. Every customer is different, but thanks to metrics you'll be able to determine how efficient your campaigns are. You'll be able to decide on which emails are working the best and which ones are underperforming. So, don't worry too much about getting your email campaign perfect at the beginning, because really, it's a game of adjusting as you go alone. You make changes here or there, fixing and improving your performance with each email that you send.

Avoid Purchasing Leads

When you're just getting started, you may come across some services offering to sell you high-quality email leads. They have proprietary email lists in X field, and for a small (or large) fee, it can all be yours, to do with as you please. The problem with these lead lists is that there is no way to verify if these leads are any good. Most of the time, they are just old emails collected through the years by some big data collector. There is no guarantee that these leads would be high quality or even remotely interested in getting emails from you.

Most of the time, these email lists are just pieces of junk being sold by hucksters looking to make a quick buck online. A lot of times, they have collected the data from some company, having paid pennies for a few thousand useless emails. Customers will not respond to those emails and chances are, most of them are just email accounts made for collecting spam anyway.

The fact is, there is nothing that will replace your own efforts and energy when it comes to generating high-quality leads. Yes, it might take more time, and yes, it can be more expensive in terms of advertising costs, but at the end of the day, each lead that you generate on your own is yours to keep for as long as you want. You won't incur any additional marketing fees to send emails straight to these leads. That is well worth the price of admission.

Quiz

1. What makes an email list so important?
   a. You can directly market to consumers
   b. Collected emails can be sold for cash
   c. Consumers love to sign up for stuff
   d. Both B and C
2. How often should you ask for emails from visitors?
   a. Only once
   b. As often as you can,
   c. Three to four times
   d. Never
3. What is a lead magnet?
   a. A product or service that consumers get in exchange for their emails
   b. A type of Facebook ad
   c. A physical product that is sold on your website
   d. None of the above
4. What kind of emails should be sent to customers?
   a. Newsletters
   b. Product promotions
   c. Content promotions
   d. All of the above
5. Customers don't care if they receive spam or not
   a. True
   b. False

Chapter 11: What affiliate marketing strategies can you employ?

Once you have the basics all put together, it's time for you to start focusing on strategy. A good, effective strategy can give you an edge, improving the value of your website and increasing sales. Remember, a goal is not a strategy. Sure, you might have an end number in mind, some idea of how much money you want to make in the long run, but just because you have a goal doesn't mean you have the necessary methods to reach that goal.

This chapter will focus on a few different strategies that you can use as you work towards reaching your goals as an affiliate marketer. Let's take a look at a few different methods that can help sharpen and improve both customer experiences and your sales.

Track the movement of your users

By using a tracking system known as a heatmap, you can follow the real-time activity of users on your website. You can see where their mouse movements have been, creating pockets of "heat" on your screen, the hotter areas on the screen are the ones that have the most amount of mouse attention. A heatmap will help you capture the most accurate picture of what exactly users are interested in on your website. You can use this information to produce more content that is similar to the hottest parts of your report, as well as delivering less content in areas that are running cold.

A heatmap also helps you understand conversions as well. If you notice that a specific banner ad or affiliate link has a tremendous amount of heat, but little amounts of actual clicks, something might be wrong. Either you are not presenting the right kind of advertisement for these links, the graphic isn't engaging enough, or there is some other factor that is holding them back from at least clicking.

While you can learn a lot from heatmaps, following the movement of your users, you won't' be able to directly figure out why they engage with specific types of content more than others. You simply can't ask them their thoughts and opinions. The only thing that you can do is infer from the data points, and come to your own conclusions. But still, the value of a heatmap is incredibly high. It will give you the ability to adapt and react to how people are viewing your website from day today!

Finding a heatmap service isn't too difficult either. There are plenty of online services that offer the use of free heatmaps, as well as ones that offer paid upgrades to get access to better metrics. It's really just a matter of finding the software that is right for you.

Judge Each Affiliate Based on Their Landing Page

One important thing to keep in mind is that when you're selling affiliate products, people who click on the links will be directed away from your website and onto the advertiser's landing page. This means that there are certain things that are out of your hands, thing such as web designed and good ad copy. So while you might have a brilliant website with good copy and design, your affiliate landing page might not be that good looking. If that's the case, it could quickly turn off your customers when they land.

So it's important that you judge each affiliate based on their landing page. Do you best to find products with functional, well-designed landing pages, or else you may end up having most of your efforts wasted. Fortunately, most advertisers know that this is an essential part of the equation, so they are willing to spend their time and energy on creating excellent landing pages, but every now and then you may end up coming across a business that isn't paying any attention to web design. If that's the case, you will most likely want to avoid selling those products, even if they fit your niche perfectly.

Understand factors that affect landing page conversion rates

There are a lot of things that can affect landing page conversion rates. Whether it's on your website or your advertisers, customers are looking for specific results when browsing online. The first and biggest one is the loading speed. The average customer is only willing to wait about 2 seconds for a website to finish loading. After 3 seconds, you're looking at a loss rate of nearly 40% of your traffic! So you will need to spend time working and monitoring on your website loading speeds. Make sure that you do everything in your power to get the website to load as quickly as possible. Spend some time studying what type of plugins you'll need to get a fast loading speed. Then, make sure that you are using a speed tester online, such as Google Speed Test, to determine how fast your site loads across different parts of the country and the world. These testers are often able to pinpoint what areas are causing the most amount of problems for you in terms of loading speed, giving you an idea of what you need to fix.

Another thing to consider with landing page conversion rates is cost. You can't expect that every single person who lands on your landing page will make a conversion because people are naturally averse to spending money. So, keep that factor in mind as you look at your conversion rates. Higher price points will cause lower levels of conversion, whereas lower price points can increase your chances of conversion. Of course, you can't choose what the prices are for these products, so don't fret too much. Just know to have realistic expectations based around the cost of the products that you are selling.

Ad copy is the next most significant part of a landing page conversion rate. You'll want to create ad copy that sells, copy that motivates them enough to click the buy button right now. This isn't the easiest of tasks, but it will be made much easier if you have a good, well-written copy. Usually, you will want to focus as tightly as possible on one single product. Dividing attention on a landing page is never a good idea because it increases the chance of the consumer becoming paralyzed by the choices in front of them. Instead, create a landing page that focuses on one and only one product at a time. You might need to create five different landing pages if you are selling five different products, but that's a good thing! Keeping your products divided from each other means that each reader is entirely captivated by the single product in front of them. Keep all ad copy focused on the virtues and benefits of the individual product and you will see a higher rate of conversions than if you were just offering a large variety of options on a single page.

Focus on high-quality traffic for your landing pages

Remember, you want high-quality traffic more than anything else out there. This means that you want people who are specifically in your target market visiting your landing pages. Why? Because people within your niche are the ones, who will actually convert! People who are outside of the niche won't save, and even if they do, the cost of getting them to switch is significantly higher than people inside of your target market.

Think about it. What is more natural, to get a fisherman to go fishing, or to take someone who hates the outdoors and convince them to go on a fishing trip with you? Time and energy are limited resources in the entrepreneurial world. You don't want to waste all of your energy and efforts on people who will never convert. Therefore, it is of the utmost importance that you focus only on directing high-quality traffic to your landing pages.

So what does this mean in practical terms? It means giving up the notion that you want as many people as possible to visit your website. Instead, you want as many high-quality individuals as you can to visit your website. You can encourage these high-quality visits by ensuring that your traffic sources are always related to your target niche. Work to keep your content consistently focused only on your niche. In other words, stay in your lane as much as possible. Don't create incentives for low-quality visitors to head over to your website. This means tightening up your advertising so that it is highly targeted.

Quiz

1. What is a heatmap?
    a. A visual depiction of clicks and attention your website
    b. A map of temperatures in the United States
    c. A type of marketing ploy
    d. An advertising campaign
2. What is the most essential part of a good landing page?
    a. Good ad copy
    b. A high-quality picture of the product
    c. Both A and B
    d. Fast loading times
3. Any traffic is good traffic
    a. True
    b. False
4. What makes a visitor high quality?
    a. They are part of your target demographic
    b. They came from a social media reference
    c. They indiscriminately purchase products with little research
    d. All of the above

Chapter 12: How to succeed in affiliate marketing

Success in affiliate marketing is possible, as long as you are willing to put in the time and effort. The first step to reaching major success is to define exactly what you would consider success. Do you want $2,000 a month in sales? $5,000? $10,000? All of these are possible but will require ironclad discipline as well as serious dedication. And in many of these cases, it will require a significant amount of time to pass before you are able to reach these milestones. But they are possible. As long as you are willing to treat this as a real job and focus your energy as much as possible on good business practices, you will eventually be able to reach your goal. Let's look at some ways that you can bolster your success as an affiliate marketer.

Sell goods and services that you are knowledgeable about

One of the easiest ways to boost your sales is to simply stick to products that you have a serious passion about. The more you understand about a product, the more you will have an eye for marketing, and most importantly, the more you will be able to answer questions and anticipate hesitation. We've already talked about this before in previous chapters, but it bears repeating here. If you are able to tap into your own passion and love for a product, you will have a greater chance of selling that product to other people, because your passion will translate across the pages. Conversely, if you are selling a product that you genuinely don't care about and find to be bothersome, that energy will slow you down.

Keep your online assets active

Whether it's your blog, your mailing list or your social media platforms, you have to remember that movement is one of the most important things. There are so many diversions on the internet that most people will quickly stop paying attention to a product or a website if there isn't much activity. Keep a rigid content schedule for all areas of your online assets. Be it Facebook, Instagram or a simple email campaign. You want to be as active as possible so that people don't forget about you. In this online economy, being forgotten, even for a few weeks, could potentially cost you in sales!

Use Tools And Programs to aid you

Once you start getting into the groove of affiliate marketing, you should look for tools and plugins that can assist you in your work. Content management systems like WordPress are incredibly flexible and offer a ton of great third-party plugins that can enhance your affiliate marketing system. Whether it's an ad manager, a contact form system or even just an improved analytics program, you can significantly increase your efficiency by using these tools.

However, it is essential to take note that a tool and program cannot replace the basics of affiliate marketing. Be cautious when it comes to accepting the claims of specific programs that they can help you make tens of thousands a month, just by signing up for their service. Oftentimes, these programs are expensive and are really just looking to take advantage of people who are looking for fast shortcuts. As a rule, a good tool or program enhances your affiliate marketing efforts; it doesn't simply "generate cash fast." Avoid anyone who claims or has guarantees about profits seen from using their products. Oftentimes these people tend to make their money just from selling their products, not actual affiliate marketing.

Avoid Blackhat Tactics

Blackhat is a term that refers to using loopholes and exploits in systems, as well as outright hacking. In your time studying affiliate marketing, you may come across people who claim that they have brilliant black hat tactics that will increase your sales tenfold. They often point to some kind of sketchy exploit or blatantly unethical tactic that may increase your sales in the short term. The problem with blackhat practices is twofold. The first is that it simply violates the rules of ethical behavior, taking illegal or immoral shortcuts will affect your credibility down the line.

The second problem is that affiliate networks are often familiar with the many different exploits that black hat affiliate marketers try to use. Since they are so wise to these methods, they will quickly be able to determine if you are engaging in unethical behavior and will cut off your profits as soon as possible. Some might even consider litigation, as blackhat methods are a breach of their terms and conditions.

So, if you are looking for ways to increase your sales and come across a freelancer who is offering blackhat services in exchange for a fee, it would be best to steer clear of them. The worst case scenario is that they are a scammer, just looking to make a buck, and the best case scenario is that you make a few sales and then get your accounts shut down by your affiliate program.

Don't stop with one website

Once you've seen success with your first website, you may want to consider starting another one. The fact is, the potential for making money on each niche can be limited since there is only a small pool of customers compared to larger, more extensive interests. While a niche can provide you with willing customers who will make these purchases, you will eventually reach a limit of how much you can make. Ultimately, the cost of acquiring new customers will grow too expensive, and you'll have diminishing returns in your marketing efforts.

This isn't always the case, but you never know. There may be a chance that at some point in the future, your current website strategy will begin to waver. Either taste change or more competition arrives, leaving you in the dust.

Just like with investing in the stock market, you don't want just to put all of your eggs in one basket and wait for your investment to take off.

Diversification is a great way to protect your assets and ensure that you won't suddenly lose out on a large amount of monthly income.

Creating multiple sites also has the potential for significantly increasing your revenue. If you find two or three different niches that are all profitable, you could double or triple your monthly profits, just by running and maintaining all three websites at the exact same time. This isn't the easiest thing in the world to pull off, but it is indeed worth it!

So when is it a good time for you to begin creating that second affiliate site? Once you are making a steady profit off of your first website. By then, you will have all the necessary experience in creating and operating a niche website that opening up a second one won't be nearly as difficult as the first one. But remember, you cannot approach making a second website lightly. You must take it as seriously as you have taken the first one. If you are able to take it seriously, you will see your profits begin to climb even higher as you collect monthly revenue from two different sites!

Learn to cross-sell related products

A good blog post can actually sell a group of different products at the same time. Some products can be related to each other indirectly, especially if they are part of the same niche. Creating a content strategy that is designed to incorporate a multitude of different products to the same customer is known as cross-selling. Some marketers are able to integrate cross-selling by creating shopping guides or product checklists for specific activities. While it is essential to keep your landing pages nice and separate, it's a different game on your basic blog pages. A broader net on your less targeted content may result in a higher level of sales, as customers who have already bought product A may take a look at products B and C, which are related to product A in some way and realize that they want it.

Create a core team to grow your business

As your profits climb, you should seriously consider taking on more people to join your team. Once you are able to pay them an hourly wage out of the profits that you are making, you will be in a good position. Why spend the money on team members? Simply put, the more people who are working with you, the more value is being brought to your business, which in turn allows for you to increase your profit levels even higher.

Scaling a business requires more manpower. You simply cannot do it alone. Well, you could, but you would be spending a lot of time and burning yourself out on specific tasks that just about anyone could do. A good entrepreneur learns how to hire out other people so that they can focus on what really matters for the business. Sure, you might be able to "save" money by not hiring additional people, but you are also limiting your income potential.

Suppose, for example, that instead of operating a second niche website by yourself, you were to hire a manager who handles all of the content production for the second site. You do all of the work in getting everything set up, you do the niche research, you put together the business plan, but you pay someone a wage to do all of the days to day operations. Now, you're freed up to focus mostly on your first website, while they are busy working to make your second website profitable. Then on top of that, they get a wage, while you are the one who reaps the majority of the profits for the second website! This has now increased your income significantly, but your workload has remained relatively the same!

Hiring additional workers to join your core team is worth it, as long as you are able to pay for them out of your profits. This will help reduce the number of expenses that you are paying out of pocket. The last thing that you want to do is to go in the negatives because you have taken on staff at the wrong time. If your affiliate marketing business is going well, then you should be able to support staff off of those profits. If you aren't performing up to that level yet, think twice before going further in the hole and shelling out of pocket for more staff.

Of course, there is one exception to this rule, and that is if you find yourself without the necessary skills for a significant part of the affiliate marketing business model. For example, if you aren't a good writer, you will certainly need to hire someone who is skilled so that they can generate sound and useful content for your website. These costs are just part of the initial investment required when it comes to affiliate marketing. Otherwise, wait until you have made some profits before you take on more talent.

Reinvest profits into your business

As you begin to see profits, you have two choices. You can pocket the money, enjoying the fruit of your labors and spend it as you please. Or you can take a portion of those profits and reinvest them in the business. This will help significantly with scaling up, increasing your advertising costs and overall bringing in higher income potential. But you want to be careful here, as you should still reap some of the rewards for what you have done. Find an ideal ratio of how much you want to pocket and how much you want to reinvest. Don't reinvest all of your money, as there is no guarantee you'll see a return. If that's the case and you don't see any gains, you basically just wasted all of your time on this endeavor. Taking a portion for yourself will help keep you motivated and focused on expanding your income potential even more. But don't take too much! You will still want to grow your business as much as you can, so try to find an ideal ratio. A good rule of thumb would be to reinvest at least half of what you earn and pocket the rest. This will allow you to scale up rather quickly, while also keeping a piece of the profits for yourself to do with as you please.

Renegotiate terms with the advertiser

Advertisers are looking to make sales. Their primary goal is to see publishers sell as many products as they can so that they can make a large portion of profit for mostly doing nothing. They reward the publisher with a commission, and both parties are satisfied. At the beginning of the relationship with the advertiser, they hold all of the power. They are the ones who have the right to say yes or no to working with you. They set the terms because you have no credibility in their eyes. More importantly, they are able to set up the deal so that it works in their favor. This means they take the majority of the profits and leave you with a smaller commission. This is fair because until you prove yourself, they have no incentive to pay you a higher commission.

However, just because you have made the original deal doesn't mean it has to stay that way forever. Once you start selling enough products, you will be able to display not only your credibility with your advertisers but also your salesmanship. Each sale that you bring in for them makes them more productive and therefore, happier. If you start to sell a large enough amount of these products, the power structure will begin to shift. You will have a more considerable amount of influence with the advertiser because you are earning for them and bringing in a ton of sales. This gives you enough weight to renegotiate your commission structure with them.

Some advertisers might simply say no, but a good one will know that you have the ability to deliver results. Since you don't have to work exclusively with them and could select any other advertiser you like, they will want to retain your services. Once you have a proven track record and display that you can bring in a lot of sales, you should try to renegotiate your terms so that the commissions are more favorable. The worst that can happen is that they just say no. The best that can happen is that they recognize your efforts and give you a larger slice of the pie. This increases your bottom line without any additional work on your half!

On top of that, once you have a proven track record, you can take your data and bring it to the more discerning affiliate programs. This will grant you access to potentially higher quality advertisers and better commission structures as well as better products to sell. In other words, if you can prove yourself through hard work and determination, the options and possibilities for making money increase exponentially.

Don't just create websites, create brands

Anyone can create a website. You just need an afternoon and access to Wordpress. A website by itself is nothing special. What makes a website special is the branding attached to it. A good brand has a strong visual identity that is present in all of the content that they create. Usually, a simple type of logo or an iconic lettering style will help customers come to recognize your brand. Then, whenever they come across content that you've created, they will quickly recognize your brand. If they have positive feelings towards your brand, such as trust, this increases the chances of them interacting with your content. Better yet, it may also remind them of certain products that they came across earlier, and will motivate them to return to your site and make a purchase.

A brand is a combination of attitude, style, and colors. Each website that you create for your affiliate marketing should have a strongly defined brand. Pick a primary, secondary and tertiary color for your brand, then make sure that you only use those colors on your website. This may seem small at first, but colors are how we primarily recognize brands. Think about the colors of Coca-Cola; all you need to do is see the familiar red and white, and instantly, you're thinking about coke before you even see the words.

You will want to have a logo as well. Something custom made and striking, able to quickly capture the attention of someone who glances at your content, either through social media sharing or through an ad. These logos are essential because they will allow you to watermark your content. With the nature of online sharing, there will be people who take visual content of yours and begin to circulate it, neglecting to include links back to your site. This isn't a necessarily malicious act, as a matter of fact, most people tend to do this. By having a logo watermarked onto your visual content, people will become aware of your brand and if they like what you have made, will look up your brand, bringing them to your website.

The last piece of brand identity is attitude. Every brand projects some kind of image, some sort of idea meant to evoke an emotion or feeling. This is one of the more intangible parts of branding, but it is necessary if you want people to have a loyalty to your website that goes beyond simply liking your products. Attitude can be conveyed by sharing your unique vision to the world on your about page. It can be found in the way you write about specific topics, and how you share your feelings on issues. If you want to convey a funloving, sports kind of lifestyle, then you'll want all of your content to reflect that attitude. If you are working as primarily as a business to business website, then you will want to keep a professional tone. Attitude will help you stay on brand and more importantly, keep your tone consistent across the board.

Quiz

1. When is the best time to start a second website?
    a. Immediately after you make the first one
    b. Once you start seeing profit from your first one
    c. Never
    d. After a few years
2. What makes diversification so necessary for affiliate marketing?
    a. Market tastes may change at any moment, diminishing your sales
    b. Affiliate companies want to see a publisher with multiple websites
    c. Income can potentially be doubled by adding more sites to your portfolio
    d. Both A and C
3. How much profit should you reinvest in your business in the beginning?
    a. All of it
    b. Half
    c. 10%
    d. None
4. When you have made a deal with an advertiser, there is no way to change the terms later on
    a. True

b. False
5. What makes for a good brand?
    a. Recognizable colors
    b. A good logo
    c. Consistency in tone
    d. All of the above

Chapter 13: How to Increase Your Web Traffic

Traffic is the lifeblood of your website. You're going to need to find steady ways to generate it on a daily basis, especially if you want to make as many sales as possible. Let's look at some of the most time-tested ways that you can increase your web traffic.

Guest Posting

Guest posting is one of the easiest ways of increasing your traffic. All you need to do is find a blog that is writing in the same niche that you are writing in and contact them. Ask if they would be willing to host one of your pieces on their website, or if they would be interested in writing for your blog. Either way, you'll be able to increase your chances of generating traffic by tapping into that blog's userbase. Then, a portion of those readers will then convert to following your blog and over time, you will see a steady uptick in traffic.

Not all niche blogs will be interested in guest posting. Some may be direct competitors to you and will most likely not be open to having you write on their website, as it would direct traffic away from their sales. Make sure that the blogs that you target are not directly competing with you. There are plenty of fan websites out there that are run by people who just simply enjoy talking about the niche without any sales angle. Those are the ones that have the best chance of working with you as a guest blogger.

Guest appearances

If you have put a good amount of time and energy into creating good, solid content for your website, you may be able to position yourself as an authority on that subject. If that's the case, you can reach out to video blogs, YouTube channels or podcasts that cover these niche topics and see if they would be willing to host you to talk about a specific issue. This can be a great way of both getting your name out there and directing traffic back to your website. And besides, in today's content starved world, most content creators are always looking for new stuff. An interview or guest co-host to one of their shows is just another way to expand their content, so they will most likely be open to having you on.

Search Engine Optimization

SEO is one of the most important tools when it comes to generating traffic. In fact, of all the tools that we are talking about in this chapter, SEO is the single most important one you can use. SEO allows people to organically come across your website when searching for terms related to your niche. Good SEO means that you will show up at the top of the search engine lists, showing up on the front page of Google or Bing. Bad SEO means that you won't be discovered at all, no matter how relevant your website is to their searches.

Search engine optimization isn't terribly hard to do, but it does require a lot of education on the matter. SEO practices are constantly changing, and there are always new things that you can learn about the subject matter. If you want to be successful as an affiliate marketer, make no mistake, you absolutely must learn SEO. Fortunately, there are so many tools and resources online that you will have no problem learning all of the best practices for the current year.

Don't make the mistake of thinking that SEO is optional. People overwhelmingly using search engines to find new websites. Think about how often you use Google or another search engine. You most likely use these websites on a daily basis, just so you can find the content that is relevant to your questions. Search engine optimization will allow for your website to show up closer to the front page which will naturally increase the flow of traffic that you need in order to survive. So, spend the necessary time learning everything about best SEO practices and then apply them as much as you can. You will make far more sales than if you were just to leave it alone.

Another thing to note of is that you will undoubtedly come across services that offer SEO optimization. These costly services will often make all sorts of promises about increasing your rankings, getting you a substantial amount of traffic, etc. It would be best to steer clear of these services until you have a good, clear understanding of SEO. Most of these services offer either basic level assistance but charge quite a bit for it, or worse, use unethical and inefficient methods of increasing your rankings in the short term. Sure, there are some legitimate services out there that will help with SEO, but ultimately you will need a conventional understanding of the practice before you are able to determine what services you actually need. You can do most SEO stuff yourself and save a fortune in the process.

Marketing in forums and other communities

Online forums are an excellent place for people interested in specific niches to come together and discuss various topics about the said niche. As a marketer, you might be able to find a natural home in these communities, sharing exciting ideas and fostering dialogue about your products. However, just like with social media, marketing through forums takes a subtle, gentle hand. The whole goal isn't just to sell as much as you can to people through these forums. Most folks would take one look at a poster like that and know to ignore them for good.

You must be willing to participate in these forums as not just a marketer, but also as a member. Talk about things other than your own business, ask questions, share ideas and content that doesn't belong to you. In other words, be a participating member of the community who wants to add value to the lives of others. You can put your important links in your signature so that when you make a post, people will always be able to visit your links, even if you aren't specifically talking about your own business. This is a better way to promote your products passively and won't annoy anyone.

Using ads to get traffic

Paid advertisements are one of the most surefire ways to generate traffic. Thanks to the power of marketing systems like Google Adwords and Facebook marketing, you will be able to target particular demographics, the types of people who would be interested in the products that you have to sell. All you need is to spend some time learning how to use ads, create a budget and then you'll be good to go. You want to run ads as much as you can afford, as that is one of the surest ways to increase your traffic. Not only will you improve your traffic with paid ads, but the traffic will also be of higher quality since the advertising systems are targeted. This increases the chance of getting followers who will repeatedly visit your website.

Free versus paid traffic

Free traffic can be excellent since, after all, it is free, but the fact is, most of the time free traffic will be of a lower quality than paid traffic. Why is this? Because free traffic is untargeted. There are many things that can drive a person to visit your website, and if they didn't click on an ultra-targeted ad meant to arrive in front of only a specific group of people, there is a chance the traffic may be low quality.

On the other hand, targeted ads bring in only the highest quality of readers, since you have worked to create ads that would interest them in seeing more of your content. This isn't always the case, as you may end up having a few low-quality leads slip in through the cracks, but for the most part, paid traffic is more focused than free traffic.

As you build your marketing strategies, however, you may find yourself focusing on more and more methods of generating free traffic. The appeal of free is very significant, after all, if you don't pay for traffic and you get some conversions, you basically got free money, right? While that may be true, don't be fooled. Paid methods of generating traffic are far more efficient than free methods. Why is this? Because with ad systems you are only paying for results. You only pay when someone clicks the link leading into your website. You have metrics with paid advertising, the ability to see how well campaigns are doing. With free advertising, you have no such metrics. You merely put content out there, create the SEO and hope for the best. Over time, you'll be able to analyze where your traffic is coming from and see which methods are working, but there is a large amount of guesswork involved.

At the end of the day, free traffic is helpful, but you cannot rely on it to do the heavy lifting. Any business endeavor requires a financial investment. When you are brand new, the opportunities for free traffic will be few and far inbetween. You will want to pay to bring in as much new traffic as you can afford. This will help boost your initial following at the beginning and will ultimately lead to higher levels of sales. Don't rely solely on free traffic. It simply doesn't have the same power as paid advertising. Yes, it costs more, but it will generate you more revenue.

Tracking Success and Refining Campaigns

As you run ad campaigns, you will see varying results, depending on the types of ad that you ran, how big the budget was, the target audience, etc. One of the more useful features of modern online advertising systems like Facebook is the ability to refine your campaigns as you go along. Each time that you run an ad campaign, you will learn a plethora of valuable information. You'll be able to analyze your conversion rate and see how much it cost to convert each customer.

You may find at the beginning that your ad campaigns aren't very efficient. Either the cost of customer acquisition is too high, or you only don't see any conversions. Don't be discouraged! The more you run ads, the more you will be able to refine your campaigns and improve your targeting. Treat each ad run as an experiment. If a run fails or doesn't provide the results that you were looking for, take that data into consideration and make changes. Make a few tweaks at a time, until finally, you are able to determine what wasn't performing correctly. You may find that all you need to do to fix an ad run is to get a better image for your ad.

Metrics and data analysis are vital to running proper ad campaigns. And you can only get those metrics by running campaigns. Don't try to get them perfect, right out of the gate. Instead, adopt an attitude of constant refinement. Refine, refine, refine, until finally, you are able to produce high-functioning ads that product a lot of good results. This may be costly at first, but it is really just the price of doing business. Once you are able to find that sweet spot in your ads, you will be able to generate far more revenue than you lost.

Starting your First Campaign

Running your first ad campaign might be a bit intimidating, but don't worry! The goal is to learn how to maximize results through repeated testing. Instead of trying to get it perfectly the first time, just focus on learning the fundamentals. Spend as much time as you can reading up about the best ways to improve your ad copy, what images work best for ads and which ad systems that you want to use. Then, put in a small amount of money, just for a test run. You don't want to spend a few hundred dollars on an ad that isn't going to convert. Instead, aim small first, see if you can get some results with just a few dollars, maybe 5 or 10, and then adjust as you go along. If you notice that your ad is performing well, congratulations! All you need to do is scale up, and you'll be fine. But if you find that your ad isn't doing that great, just keep on tweaking it until it does. It's better to spend $100 on 10 ad runs than it is to spend $100 on a single ad run in the beginning. Just keep track of the results and make changes each time, until you are getting exactly what you're looking for.

Utilize Ad Retargeting

Sometimes a customer looks at your ad, visits your site and then pokes around, looking at what you have to offer and the leaves without making a purchase. This is unfortunate, but it is to be expected. Most of your traffic won't convert initially. There are a lot of reasons why they don't. The first could be that they simply became distracted. Something else captured their attention and they left your site, promising that they'd come back and take a look at it later. Sometimes they just didn't have the funds to make the purchase.

If these are the cases, then not all is lost! With the help of websites like Facebook, you can actually retarget these individuals and continue to market to them. Since they've already engaged with your website the first time, it means that they are already open to what you are offering. All you need to do is run a retargeting ad and hope to see some kind of action on their behalf.

Retargeting simply requires that you have a Facebook pixel installed on your website. This pixel is a cookie that will track the behavior of the consumer. You'll be able to tell if they have converted or not, as well as monitor the other responses that they took. Once they leave the

Facebook page, you'll be able to create an audience using that pixel, retargeting the individuals who visited but didn't convert.

Setting up a pixel isn't hard to do, as Facebook offers them for free. All you need to do is install a proper app onto your WordPress or other content management system, and Facebook will automatically begin monitoring the traffic of those who come in from your ads. This will allows you to not only create retargeting ads but also create lookalike audiences, expanding your target market.

Is retargeting worth it? Absolutely! As we stated before, there are plenty of reasons that someone would opt out of making a purchase immediately. If they don't have the funds, or time to look into the product right now, they might have that availability later on. All they need is a simple reminder. If they don't engage with your retargeted ad, you know that you won't' be able to convert them again. However, if they engage with your ad, it actually significantly increases their chances of making a purchase! Retargeting is a marketer's best friend!

Quiz

1. Which traffic is best for when you're first starting out?
   a. Paid traffic
   b. Free traffic
   c. Social Media Traffic
   d. Referral traffic
2. What is the best practice for marketing on forums?
   a. Create a signature with links to your content
   b. Try to sell as much as you can to anyone who will listen
   c. Focus on answering questions and providing assistance to others
   d. Both A and C
3. What does SEO stand for?
   a. Search Engine Optimization
   b. Selling, Expanding and Organizing
   c. Serious Entrepreneurs Only
   d. Search Engine Online
4. You have to get your first ad run exactly right
   a. True
   b. False
5. What is ad retargeting?
   a. Targeting people who have already visited your website with ads

b. Refining the ad process so that it works better
c. Both A and B
d. Spending less on ads through better SEO practices.

Conclusion

Affiliate marketing has tremendous, near unlimited potential, as long as you are willing to put in the time and effort. This isn't a get rich quick scheme, but rather it is a time tested, proven method of making income online. All you need to do is stay committed, find a good niche and spend as much time as you can creating both good content and customer experiences. As long as you keep that up, you'll make plenty of cash online! Good luck out there!

Quiz Answers

Below is the answer key to the quiz sections of the book. The answers are enhanced in bold.

Chapter 1:

1. The name of the company that actually sells the product is called:
   a. Publisher
   b. Advertiser
   c. Seller
   d. Retailer
2. Affiliate marketing has a tremendous start-up cost
   a. True
   b. False(Most of the time, you can start an affiliate marketing endeavor on a shoestring budget!)
3. What is the publisher's role in affiliate marketing?
   a. Purchase the product
   b. Create links to products in the hopes of seeing a sale

    c. Buy a product and then resell it on their own website

4. A publisher collects a commission when
   a. **The customer engages in a specific action (buying or clicking a link)**
   b. The customer visits the publisher's website
   c. The customer shares the publisher's content.

Chapter 2:

1. What is high ticket affiliate marketing
   a. Selling expensive products
   b. Collecting large commissions
   c. **Both A and B**
   d. Generating a large amount of traffic
2. Customers are more reluctant to make high-cost purchases
   a. **True**
   b. False
3. You cannot make money selling low ticket items
   a. True
   b. **False (You can absolutely make money selling low ticket items, you just need to focus more on volume.)**

Chapter 3:

1. A website isn't necessary for successful affiliate marketing
   a. True
   b. **False (While it technically is possible, there is no reason for you to start affiliate marketing without a website.)**
2. Affiliate programs are often looking for
   a. Web traffic
   b. Sales results
   c. Credibility
   d. **All of the above**
3. What is most necessary to be successful in affiliate marketing?
   a. **A professional attitude (Remember, the only real way to make money in this business is to treat it exactly like a business! Half-measures won't get you anywhere!)**
   b. A nice looking website
   c. Traffic
   d. All of the above

Chapter 5:

1. When starting out, I automatically qualify for the best commission rate
   a. True
   b. **False (When starting out, you don't have an established track record, so you will, unfortunately, have to accept less than stellar commission rates.)**
2. What qualities does a good advertiser have?
   a. Good products
   b. Well designed websites
   c. Low prices
   d. **Both A and B**
3. How can you determine if an affiliate program is trustworthy?
   a. Check their own website
   b. **Look to third-party reviews (Always be sure to make sure that the third-party review isn't receiving some kind of kickback for the recommendations, or else their presentations could be compromised!)**
   c. Trust your gut
   d. Just try it and see if it works out

Chapter 6:

1. What are the three primary types of content?
   a. **Education, Inspiration, and Entertainment**
   b. Infographics, Videos and Blog Posts
   c. Facebook, Instagram, and Twitter
   d. Education, Entertainment, and Information
2. Consistency is unimportant when it comes to content scheduling
   a. True
   b. **False**
3. If you aren't good at writing, you should
   a. Give up
   b. **Hire a writer (Hiring a writer can be cheap and easy. Hopefully you don't consider the other two options!)**
   c. Steal other content and repackage it as your own
   d. Both A and C
4. Why is content so important?
   a. It drives traffic to your website
   b. It establishes authority on a niche
   c. It has the potential for generating sales
   d. **All of the Above**

Chapter 7:

1. Social media is best for
    a. Creating relationships with fans and followers
    b. Selling products constantly
    c. Sharing content
    d. Both A and C
2. The best platform to use is
    a. Facebook
    b. Twitter
    c. Snapchat
    d. The platform your target demographic uses the most
3. People want to be sold to when using social media
    a. True
    b. False (Remember, people are inundated with marketing efforts constantly. The last thing they want to deal with when using social media are sales pitches.)

Chapter 8:

1. How important are analytics for your business?
   a. **Extremely important (If you don't track your performance, how will you know if you're ever doing better? Prioritize analytics and make a point to monitor them every week!)**
   b. Moderately important
   c. Somewhat important
   d. Not important at all
2. Exaggeration is perfectly fine when it comes to marketing
   a. True
   b. **False**
3. Shiny Object Syndrom means
   a. **Constantly getting distracted by new ideas**
   b. Wanting to make more money online
   c. Fascination with mirrors
   d. Learning new methods of marketing
4. The best way to work as an affiliate marketer is alone
   a. True
   b. **False**

Chapter 9:

1. What is the best subject for a niche?
   a. Whatever is selling
   b. A passion, interest or hobby that you love
   c. Fishing gear
   d. All of the above
2. Why is passion important when it comes to choosing a niche?
   a. You will genuinely enjoy what you are doing
   b. You will understand more about the products you are selling
   c. You will have a better level of communication with customers
   d. All of the above
3. An underserved market means
   a. There isn't an extensive amount of options for consumers in that niche
   b. There is a low level of competition in the field
   c. Both A and B
   d. There is too much competition to break into

4. People purchase products because they have a problem they need solving
   a. **True (Remember, at the end of the day, all products are methods of solving problem. Even entertainment solves the problem of boredom.)**
   b. False

Chapter 10:

1. What makes an email list so important?
   a. **You can directly market to consumers**
   b. Collected emails can be sold for cash
   c. Consumers love to sign up for stuff
   d. Both B and C
2. How often should you directly ask for emails from visitors?
   a. **Only once (If you push too hard, you run the risk of pushing them away for good. Instead, just directly ask them once via pop-up and then leave them to find your squeeze page later.)**
   b. As often as you can,
   c. Three to four times

       d. Never

3. What is a lead magnet?

       a. A product or service that consumers get in exchange for their emails

       b. A type of Facebook ad

       c. A physical product that is sold on your website

       d. None of the above

4. What type of emails should be sent to customers?

       a. Newsletters

       b. Product promotions

       c. Content promotions

       d. All of the above

5. Customers don't care if they receive spam

       a. True

       b. False (Not only are there plenty of laws regulating spam, but most people also have the ability to unsubscribe to emails with a single click of a button. Don't tempt them into using that option on your emails!)

Chapter 11:

1. What is a heatmap?

a. **A visual depiction of clicks and attention your website**
b. A map of temperatures in the United States
c. A type of marketing ploy
d. An advertising campaign
2. What is the most important part of a good landing page?
    a. Good ad copy
    b. A high-quality picture of the product
    c. Both A and B
    d. **Fast loading times (While the other two are important, fast loading times rank number one. You simply cannot afford to lose 40% of your traffic due to slow loading times.)**
3. Any traffic is good traffic
    a. True
    b. **False**
4. What makes a visitor high quality?
    a. **They are part of your target demographic**
    b. They came from a social media referral
    c. They indiscriminately purchase products with little research
    d. All of the above

Chapter 12:

1. When is the best time to start a second website?
    a. Immediately after you make the first one
    b. **Once you start seeing profit from your first one (You don't want to jump too quickly onto a second website, but once you see profit, you should start taking steps to make a new one.)**
    c. Never
    d. After a few years
2. What makes diversification so necessary for affiliate marketing?
    a. Market tastes may change at any moment, diminishing your sales
    b. Affiliate companies want to see a publisher with multiple websites
    c. Income can potentially be doubled by adding more sites to your portfolio
    d. **Both A and C**
3. How much profit should you reinvest in your business in the beginning?
    a. All of it
    b. **Half (This is simply the best way to rapidly expand your business. Any less and you won't be able to scale**

as quickly. Any more and you risk losing your total investment, which can make your efforts at making money online nothing more than a lengthy game of roulette.)

    c. 10%

    d. None

4. When you have made a deal with an advertiser, there is no way to change the terms later on

    a. True

    b. **False (You can always attempt to increase your commissions, especially if you are a high earner)**

5. What makes for a good brand?

    a. Recognizable colors

    b. A good logo

    c. Consistency in tone

    d. **All of the above**

Chapter 13:

1. Which traffic is best for when you're first starting out?

    a. **Paid traffic**

    b. Free traffic

    c. Social Media Traffic

d. Referral traffic

2. What is the best practice for marketing on forums?

    a. Create a signature with links to your content

    b. Try to sell as much as you can to anyone who will listen

    c. Focus on answering questions and providing assistance to others

    d. Both A and C

3. What does SEO stand for?

    a. Search Engine Optimization

    b. Selling, Expanding and Organizing

    c. Serious Entrepreneurs Only

    d. Search Engine Online

4. You have to get your first ad run exactly right

    a. True

    b. False (Remember, you can try and try again until you finally have a good refined ad. Don't put too much pressure on yourself to get it right the first time.)

5. What is ad retargeting?

    a. Targeting people who have already visited your website with ads

    b. Refining the ad process so that it works better

    c. Both A and B

d. Spending less on ads through better SEO practices.